WHAT TO DO WITH A LIBERATED WOMAN

A practical primer for men who'd like to know what the new rules are.

By Shelly Roberts and Fred Hilliard, or...
Fred Hilliard and Shelly Roberts

Smuggler's Cove Publishing
107 West John Street
Seattle, Washington 98119

ISBN 0-918484-02-2.

Library of Congress Catalog Card Number
Printed in the United States of America.

Author: Shelly Roberts.
Illustrator: Fred Hilliard.

Book and Cover Design: Ben Dennis and Fred Hilliard.
Back Cover Photo: Paul Kotz, photographer for The Design Team.
Production: Sue Johnson and Eric Savage, both of
The Design Team, Seattle, WA.

Copy Consultant: Betsy Case.
Printing: Kingsport Press, Kingsport, TN.

What's a nice man like you doing in a book like this?

Hopefully learning how to be a lot more successful with the women in your life.

Certainly, it isn't your fault that somebody's changed all the rules you learned when you were growing up. But that doesn't help when you find yourself with a bad case of foot-in-mouth disease.

It's not so difficult dealing with liberated, enlightened women. If there is a single rule to be learned, it's this: Let your common, human sense, *not what your mother taught you,* dictate what you do.

Women are looking for men who respect them as people. And that goes for cheerleaders and ex-prom queens as well as corporation presidents.

If anything you're about to do, even if all the old etiquette says to do it, smacks of patronage, or results in treating the women around you as if they were pets or apendages, don't do it. If particular women in your life want some other kind of treatment, they'll let you know that. A frown when you don't open the door, or a quick disappearance to the powder room perfectly timed to the arrival of the check, will give you those clues.

But on the whole, these days, it is safer to assume that she'd rather be treated as your equal.

Now for some specifics.

In most cases, here's what to do with a liberated woman:

Table of contents.

Strictly business.

Cigarettes: a lighter subject. 9
What do you do if she offers to light your cigarette? 10
Let's shake on it. 11
Doing the elevator shuffle. 11
Are you going to stand for this? 13
Who's supposed to take notes on this meeting? 14
Who gets the coffee these days? 17
Who makes the coffee these days? 17
Who opens the door for whom? 19
The business lunch: who gets the check? 21
Don't swear to it. 22
Who do you hire, him or her? 23
Ohmygawd, she's my boss! 25
Watch your language! 26

What do you say to a secretary?

Maybe she doesn't really want your job. 28
Title shot. 29
No one should own one. 29
If you say, "Get the coffee," say it in writing. 29
Sew what? 30
Integrate! 32

Playing it single.

Would I like to go where with you? 34
Who pays for the babysitter? 35
What if she's taking karate? 36
She's not such a good sport anymore. 37
Bed time story. 39
Birth control: pregnant with possibilities. 40
Who pays for the abortion? 40

What if you're married?

What if she's having her consciousness raised? 42
Housework? Who on earth would want to do housework? 43
The bread winner and the bread baker. 45
The name game. 46
What shall we name the baby? 47
Who says staying at home isn't work? 49
Who's helping whom? 52
'Til alimony do us part. 53
Who keeps the kids? 54

The non-traditional trades.

No comment. 59
Maybe she's just in it for the money. 60
Tote that barge. Lift that bale. 60
What are you doing under my car, Lady? 61
What do you say to a woman doctor? 63
How do you talk to a woman with an odd job? 64

Something for everyone.

Give the nice lady your seat. 66
My compliments. 67
One giant step for person-kind. 68
Girls or women? Ms., Mrs., or Miss? 68
Where'd all the Broads and Chicks go? 71

STRICTLY BUSINESS

Cigarettes: a lighter subject.

To light or not to light her cigarette?

You'll just have to take our word for it about the reasons, but a lot of women think it's important, so:

The answer is mostly: No, don't.

Unless 1) you're with a woman who likes having her cigarette lit. Or, 2) she's out of matches and you're sporting your own monogrammed Zippo.

What do you do if she offers to light your cigarette?

Inhale.

Let's shake on it.

More and more women are seeing a business handshake as a sign of equal treatment.

So you should offer to shake hands.

Don't use the bone crusher you'd use to greet the flanker back from the New York Jets when he wants to sell you insurance, but use a good steady, firm pressure. She isn't going to break, and she'll appreciate the honest straightforwardness of the gesture.

Doing the elevator shuffle.

First you put your two feet close up tight, then you swing 'em to the left, and then you swing 'em to the right.

That's very close to what we're all doing daily just to ride to another floor.

First men have to get out of the way to let the women in.

Then the women have to move to the back of the elevator so there's room for the men to get in.

Then the men have to get out of the way to let the women out.

Then they have to get back on the elevator and do the same chorus at the next stop.

But it isn't necessary. Just let everyone on in order of appearance. Then get out of the way for anybody in the back who made the mistake of getting caught there when they should have been shouldering their way to the door.

No one will think that your mother didn't teach you manners. In fact, they may not even notice the difference. But this simple re-ordering of elevator priorities could save companies hundreds of work-hours a year.

And you might never have to do a two-step over somebody's umbrella, or the elevator shuffle again.

"On your mark...get set...SIT!"

Are you going to stand for this?

Should you stand up when a woman first comes into the conference room?

Sure. A lot of the time you should. But not just because she's a woman.

You should stand to welcome her if you're chairing the meeting.

You should also stand if she's the Big Boss in from corporate headquarters, your client, your newest business associate, is considerably older than you are, or just bought the Miami Dolphins for cash.

But she'll also stand for you if you meet any of the above criterion. So act like you expected it.

And don't expect her to be seated first. These days everybody sits down more or less at the same time.

Without anybody pulling out any chairs for anybody.

Who's supposed to take notes on this meeting?

Business women are advising each other not even to take a pencil into a business meeting, but to develop their memories so they won't automatically be forced into a secretarial role.

If notes need to be taken, bring in a real secretary for the task. Or borrow a tiny tape recorder. Or let every person in the room take a turn at successive meetings.

"Wait a minute!
Wait a minute, J.P.!
Did you say, 'In conclusion,
I think it imperative,'
or, 'In conclusion,
I think it essential'?"

"Think of it, Ms. Dortwhether, as a matter of simple office economics. You keep making the coffee, and I'll keep signing your pay check."

Who gets the coffee these days?

Whoever is the closest to the pot.

Who makes the coffee these days?

Most office coffee machines have gotten so simple that even an executive vice president could figure them out. So why the bruhaha over brewing?

Simple.

It looks like housework. And women are getting supersensitive about office chores that look like household chores.

If yours is an egalitarian office, then whoever arrives first should put on the pot. Same thing for whoever drank the last cup during the day.

If yours isn't an egalitarian office, then most of the time the job should fall to someone on the support staff, because it makes more sense for someone making three dollars an hour to do it, than for someone making twenty, thirty or fifty dollars an hour.

If, however, you are the expensive executive with nothing much to do at the moment, and your secretary has at least four hours' worth of stapling to do just to get your memos out to the branch offices, then you should plug in the pot. In this case, office economics works precisely in reverse.

You could also take the job away from your secretarial staff, and give it to the office errand runner or mail deliverer. They make even less an hour than secretaries.

In any case, if you expect any member of your support staff to be making coffee as part of their job description, be sure that it's actually in that job description.

Who opens the door for whom?

Same thing as with the coffee.

Whoever's the closest.

Car doors are the same. Unless she's nine months preganant, on crutches, or is still sitting in the car when you're already inside ordering your first drink.

The business lunch: who gets the check?

How do you fight it out with the men at lunch?

About the same rules apply here. It divides up according to whom you're with.

If you're with a co-worker, establish the ground rules on the way out the door of the office. Women co-workers know that if you're having to pick up the lunch tab all the time, you'll soon stop asking. So most of them are willing to go dutch.

If you're with a woman client, you should usually fumble the fastest. But if she really wants to catch the check, it's okay to give up after the second protest.

If you are the client, you can afford to fumble a little slower, regardless of whether your luncheon partner is a man or woman.

But if you're doing a one-on-one, the laws of reciprocation should always apply.

If everyone at the table is an equal, you can do one of two things. The first is the safest. Ask for separate checks as you sit down. Then everybody knows how much they can afford to eat.

If you're the one who's having only mineral water and a small salad with lemon juice dressing, this system could save you a bundle over the other option.

The other option is just to split the check evenly. But make sure, if you suggest this, that everyone had about the same amount of food and drink. Otherwise co-workers could suddenly develop a bad case of "Oops-I-have-a-conference-report-to-write" the next time you suggest everyone get together for lunch.

Don't swear to it.

It's not so much the "hells" and "damns" that she minds. It's the incessant apologies that almost always go with them.

She knows you wouldn't apologize if she weren't in the room.

She also knows every swear word you could possibly come up with.

She may even condone an occassional expletive as a way of expressing feeling. For herself as well as for you.

What she won't condone is the patronizing apology.

So, if you're going to feel compelled to say you're sorry, then don't give a "damn" in the first place.

Incidentally, occassional profanity might be tolerable, but obscenity, which usually refers to women's parts, is, well, obscene.

Who do you hire, him or her?

Affirmative action leans on us all.

Obviously you should hire whoever best solves your employee problem.

But don't assume that if you hire a woman, you're going to end up with a pregnant employee. You might, of course. But it's not nearly as likely as it might have been once.

And don't ask anything about marital status, potential pregnancy, or babysitting arrangements during her job interview. It's illegal. And organizations are ready and waiting to sue you on behalf of a discriminated-against woman.

Other things not to ask the women you interview: "Can you type?" or, "Do you take shorthand?"

Unless you're hiring her to type.

Or take shorthand.

"Sit down, my dear, and let's talk about your legs...er, uh...your qualifications."

Ohmygawd, she's my boss!

Female bosses are a new experience to a lot of people, but that doesn't make them just-cause for quitting.

Instead, listen to the words she's saying. If what she's asking you to do makes sense, you shouldn't have any problem.

If it doesn't make sense, you *do* have a problem. You have to decide whether to go along or fight. (But that's not a problem of having a woman boss, that's a problem of deciding if you're going to fight your boss.)

Women are getting very sensitive about their nurturing stereotype, so even if you'd go in and rap with your male boss about your life problems, be a little careful about doing it with your female boss. She may not know that it comes with the territory and think you're trying to use her as a substitute for your mom.

Continuously bringing up her family, her children, or your own (unless one of them just did the hundred yards in nine flat, or mastered pinochle at age four) might also touch another exposed nerve, so watch it there too.

Don't go on and on about her looks, clothes or appearance. With a man, you'd probably just say, "mm, new tie?" Keep it at about that level with her too.

And, for heaven's sake, don't *under any circumstances,* make any jokes about what time of the month it is. You may be a riot in the meeting. But she won't think it's funny. And when your boss doesn't think something is funny...it isn't funny.

Watch your language!

Do not, under any circumstances, use the term "Women's Lib" in the office around any one you even vaguely suspect has any involvement in it.

(If you were addressed in the kind of tone it's usually said in, you'd be offended too.)

There isn't any clearer way to find yourself wearing an invisible Male Chauvanist tag around your neck.

If you really have to say anything at all, use the term "Women's Rights Movement" or just "Women's Movement." It's politically correct at the moment. And using it will mark you as a man who's been listening.

WHAT DO YOU SAY TO A SECRETARY?

Maybe she doesn't really want your job.

Many women are secretaries because that's what they want to be. But everyone resents being treated like the "hired help" no matter what level they're working at.

What secretaries would like is to have their job treated with some dignity.

That includes regular performance evaluations, verbal acknowledgements of accomplishments, outlines of realistic expectations.

And occasionally just saying thank you could get you the Boss of the Year award from the National Secretaries Union.

"You've been under a lot of pressure, Ed. So for Gawd's Sake, take a couple of weeks off. Meanwhile, I'll do my best to stand in the breech."

Title shot.

Don't upgrade your secretary's title unless you're really going to upgrade the job and the salary.

"Administrative Assistant" isn't fooling anyone any more.

No one should own one.

There's no such thing as property rights to your secretary.

Observe her for any signs of brains, ambition or talent, and promote her out from in front of your office.

True, you might be losing someone who knows how to spell better than you do, but you might just be gaining a dynamite junior executive and an ally in the next office power war.

And at a time like that, you could use all the friends you can create.

If you say, "Get the coffee," say it in writing.

As we said in the section on making the coffee, if you expect her to put on the pot, put it in the job description.

Sew what?

Your secretary's office tasks should be ones that keep the work flowing, the product producing, and the profits piling up.

Forget the tasks your secretary has to do because you never learned to sew a simple button, or can't remember wedding anniversaries.

Occasional favors should be treated as occasional favors. And in an emergency it's okay to ask for assistance on a split seam. But those continuing jobs that turn your secretary into your office wife could lead to a very unhappy office marriage.

Integrate!

Break with tradition entirely the next time there's an opening, and hire a male secretary. Most big cities have lots of bright young men who type and take shorthand.

But expect things to be stirred up in the office. The male staff will see it as a question of their virility and the female support staff will worry about their job security. But that too shall pass. Just be careful not to promote your newest male secretary to Junior Assistant Office Traffic Coordination Manager the first time he proves he can type a letter without a gallon of correcto-fluid.

PLAYING IT SINGLE

Would I like to go where with you?

The phone rings and the voice sounds vaguely familiar. It's a woman you know, and she'd like to ask you out.

What do you do?

You ask yourself the question women have been asking for centuries, "Do I want to go out with this person?"

If the answer is yes, you say, "Sure, I'd love to."

"If the answer is no, you say, "I'm sorry, but I always wash my hair on Saturday nights." Or just be honest and say that you're sorry, but you can't.

If she had the courage to ask you for a date, then expect her to have the courage to pay for it. You could make the offer to pick up the movie tickets if your only expenses that month are for chicken pot pies and the tune-up on your vintage Jag. But if she refuses, accept gracefully.

During the date, try not to look kept.

Most men have a little trouble trying not to look nervous. Or embarrassed. Especially when she's picking up the check. But relax.

Think of yourself as participating in a sociological experiment. Pioneers are always brave.

"Sounds exciting Helen, but I've got to put my hair up."

Who pays for the babysitter?

The amount a babysitter costs may be a small sum to you, but it could be a budget buster for your date.

But she's still going to be a bit embarrassed to ask you to pick up this tab.

You'll both have a better time if she doesn't have a meter running in her head for every minute that she's out with you. Nor should she be penalized for the privilege of your company.

So if you're feeling generous, make the offer to pick up the whole thing. It will impress her if she's someone you want to see again.

If paying for the entire babysitting bill seems too much, then agree to split the cost. But work this out before you pick her up. Then she'll know in advance how much time she can afford to spend with you, and whether she and the kids will have to eat macaroni and chicken necks for a week because she decided to see you and a movie.

What if she's taking karate?

It's a civilized sport.

One that teaches infinite control.

And she probably took it as a defense against rapists.

If she thinks that's what you are, then we recommend that you let all your muscles go lax, and look for a soft place to land.

Or ask her why she mistook you for a rapist.

She's not such a good sport anymore.

When it comes to athletic competitions, remember the lesson Bobby Riggs taught Billie Jean King, and don't expect to win.

At least not automatically.

"Eight ball. Two outta three. We'll lag for the break. Call your bank shots. Loser buys, okay?"

Bed time story.

Etchings are out.

Honesty is in.

"Oh, you're lovely, and I'd like to carry you off into the sunset," has some appeal. But straightforward seems to work a lot easier than four frustrating movie dates and a handshake at the door.

She'll respect you more if you're direct.

So if you have something in mind, and you think she's amenable, try just asking for it.

Things like: "You wanna...?" or, "How about we...?" or even "Lets!"

This is not a plea for speed, but an appeal to the end of the games.

And, of course, she also gets the right to the same courtesies. (Without getting your...er...um..."ego" deflated.)

She also should be able to say things like: "Lower," "Faster," and, "To the right."

And don't ask, "Was I any good?"

Because if you weren't, the way things are going these days, she's likely to tell you.

Birth control: pregnant with possibilities.

The pill isn't such a terrific idea any more. (Well, that's not true. It was a terrific *idea.* Until the side effects developed.)

Don't assume that the woman you're with is on them. A lot of women are choosing not to be.

Women are often being forced back to some of the old methods. But with some creative differences.

Remember the Trojan who used to live in your wallet? Well, don't be surprised if the wallet it's in is now hers.

And also don't assume that she is taking full responsibility for birth control. Some liberated women are not as sexually emancipated as others.

Find some way, between the brandy and the bedroom, to find out for sure.

Or you could find yourself rereading the chapter on who pays for the abortion.

Who pays for the abortion?

If she's under age, you've got no choice. You do. (And set some aside for a lawyer, just in case.)

If she isn't under age, but is under a severe financial handicap, like trying to live on what they pay most women these days, and all the kids in your high school class think you're the success story of 1942 or '61 or '73, then you should pay for all of it.

If you're both adults, and you both said, "Yes," then you should pay for at least half and then some.

The "then some" is for wear and tear on her body. And it should be a considerable portion. Most of her contribution to your combined abortion will be just going through with it.

WHAT IF YOU'RE MARRIED?

What if she's having her consciousness raised?

Think of it as a growth experience.

She's going to be learning some new things about the world, and seeing some things in a new light.

And, of course, that means that she'll be doing some changing.

But transitions can be tough if only one of you is changing.

So we recommend, since you're in that marriage together, that you find out if there is a men's consciousness-raising group in your city. And take it at the same time.

That way you'll both be growing in the same direction.

Housework? Who on earth would want to do housework?

It's your choice.

Split the housework and keep her.

Or.

Insist that she do it all, and lose her, then end up doing *all* the housework.

It's your choice.

The bread winner and the bread baker.

Go ahead, admit that you know how to cook.

Or learn how if you don't already know.

Since she's going to be giving up a lot of her best cooking times going to meetings, or cooking up winning schemes at the office, you should contribute your fair share of time slaving over a hot stove.

That doesn't mean that you only crank up the crockpot or break out the barbeque when company's coming. Everybody has to eat every day, so make sure your fair share is really fair.

That also doesn't mean that your night to cook is a quick trip to the chicken colonel, or a bag of burgers to go.

Besides, how many all-beef-patties-special-sauce-lettuce-cheese-pickles-onions-on-a-sesame-seed-bun can you ingest before you start wishing you could head for Mom's and a bowl of her best heartburn chili? (Forget that as an alternate plan anyway. Mom is probably out taking classes in macrame for fun and profit, or getting her PhD in anatomical microbiology.)

The name game.

First she got Daddy's name. Automatically.

Then she got yours. Automatically.

Now she'd like to have one that's all her own. It's not such an aberration if you look at it that way.

Couples are handling it any of several ways:

First there's hyphenating. Roll both names around on your tongue with hers first then with yours first and see which way sounds best.

Hyphenating says you're as proud to be with her as she is to be with you. But no cheating on this one. If you hyphenate, you *both* have to hyphenate. Just letting her say that you two are Smith-Jones, while you stay just plain Jones at the office isn't quite cricket.

Then there's each keeping your own names. It will confuse the people at the bank who print up your checks, the IRS, and your grandparents who will worry that the mail carrier will think that you're just living together. But it is a valid solution to your combined identity crisis.

A third solution is to find a third name. Just look in the phone book till you find one that you both like. It will take a bit of legal rejiggering, but at least you both start off even.

There is a fourth suggestion that's a little more radical. You take *her* name. This suggestion is particularly appealing if she happens to be an only child, and her family has a lot of money.

What shall we name the baby?

If your name solution is a composite, or if you've chosen to stay separate, there will be a problem with the little ones.

If you're a hyphenate, pass the hyphenation on to your offspring.

If you're separatists, you could let the boys have your last name, and give the girls your wife's. It'll certainly confuse all the elementary schools in the neighborhood.

Or you could let your young ones be first generation hyphenates.

Here's how it works: if you're Jones, and she's Smith, then the baby is simply Smith-Jones or Jones-Smith.

Think how happy an arrangement like that could make all the grandparents.

"Anthony? Melissa? Diogenes? Mary? Jacqueline? Bobby? Jefferson Wittinghouse, III?"

Who says staying at home isn't work?

She may be planning a cottage industry that could cause a severe change in your tax bracket, or doing more battlefield coordination of the household than any four-star general ever saw.

So if she's at home all day, your mental picture of her in a feather boa, languidly watching soap operas while you slave away at your desk, isn't exactly accurate.

When you call, don't assume that she's free to fill up half an hour of your time just because you're bored. Ask if she has the time to talk, run to the cleaners, or pick up a quick fifty board-feet of lumber from the hardware store.

If you're planning to bring someone home to dinner, let her know ahead of time. Tonight may be the night she was planning to surprise you at the door dressed in plastic wrap with or without a few strategic ribbons.

If you're not going to call first, then be prepared to serve saltines and jelly, or stop at the store yourself, and bring the food with you.

Unless you've agreed that all the household tasks are hers, something she's hardly likely to agree to in any case, don't expect that come five-fifteen, the house will be in perfect order, the children neatly brushed and cleaned, your pipe and slippers and dinner will all be waiting.

It's a nice dream, formerly fostered by old reruns of "Father Knows Best," but it just isn't likely.

1

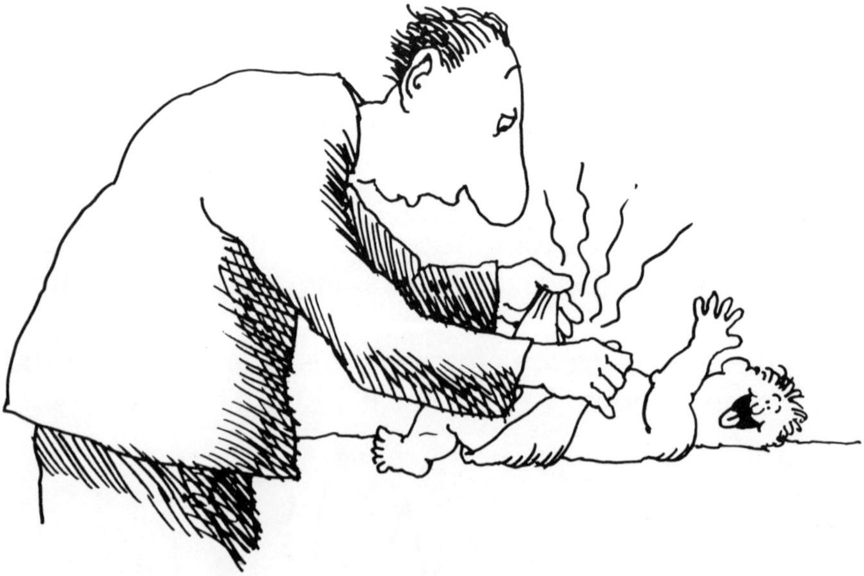

2

3

4

"She wants her Mommy."

Who's helping whom?

Offering to *"help"* with the kids, the dishes, the laundry, or any other of the household chores, tells her precisely whose job you really think it is.

So if your intention is to divide those awful tasks fairly, then do yours as though they really were yours to do.

Because *"helping"* is almost no help at all.

’Til alimony do us part.

Just because the statistics are skyrocketing, that doesn’t mean that your divorce has to be a federal case.

If you’re still speaking to each other, you should be able to work out some arrangements that benefit both of you.

Alimony is going the way of the dinosaur in all but a few states. It’s been replaced by community property or spousal support.

The operating idea in creative divorce these days is that if your wife gave up a promising career on the concert stage to care for your hearth and heart, and hasn’t touched a note since, she’s going to need some help getting to the point where she can pay her own way. That may well mean helping out financially until she’s through school: secretarial, medical or law.

There’s an exception to the just-’til-she’s-got-her-own-job rule. And that’s if it isn’t likely that she can get a job. It may be because she’s been out of the job market too long, or because she’s of an age where employers aren’t even willing to consider her. If that’s the case, you’ll just have to think of your support as deferred payment for all those years of diapers and dishes.

This isn’t any place to be practicing law without a license, so we recommend that you do what your wife should be doing, which is talking to a lawyer. But this is a much better time in the world for a man and a woman to get a working arrangement that really does work. So keep talking to each other, keep your lawyers talking to each other, and keep asking for what you think is fair.

Who keeps the kids?

The most nurturing parent should have custody.

If, for example, she's a firefighter with three days on and two days off, or she's an astronaut and can't get any time off while she's traveling on business, and you'd never consider leaving Tulsa, then you should have custody.

The decision should be based on practicality and economics. It shouldn't be based on hurt feelings or property rights to your kids.

If you can't get this one discussed objectively between the two of you, bring in a third party. If you don't, the courts just might.

A word about child support. Unlike alimony, this hasn't gone away. The parent keeping the kids is really doing the work. Bed times and traumas, first dates and discipline. So child support is a way to even up the contributions.

If you strongly suspect that your ex-wife just might actually be eating some of the food your support is supposed to be buying for the kids, so be it. She has to eat too, and you wouldn't want an undernourished human being looking after *your* kids, would you?

THE NON-TRADITIONAL TRADES

Janet's

No comment.

When you first discover that your bus driver, telphone installer, or long-haul trucker is a woman, many of the things you might have been thinking are best left unsaid.

Saying things like, “Hi, honey, what’s a pretty little thing like you doing in a job like this?” Or, “What are you tryin’ to prove, you’re a better man ’n me?” Or, “Here, Honey, a little thing like you shouldn’t be lifting something this heavy,” is not the way to her heart. It could also get you left off at the wrong street, answering a purple telephone, or accepting someone else’s shipment of widgets.

Since more and more women are entering the non-traditional trades, it should come as less and less of a surprise to find them there.

Women in non-traditional trades have already taken a lot of guff and nonsense about the jobs they’re doing, so they’ll find it most helpful if you say to them, instead, things like “Do you give transfers?” ‘Yes, we *do* want the princess phone in the bathroom,” and/or “Do you deliver to Walla Walla?”

Maybe she's just in it for the money.

Not every woman in a hard hat is a confirmed "women's libber."

Some of them just figured out that nine dollars and fifty-seven cents an hour, plus benefits, for climbing a telephone pole buys a lot more groceries than four fifty a month for drowning in a secretarial pool.

Tote that barge. Lift that bale.

If you'd normally help your five-foot-eight, one-hundred-fifty pound male co-worker lift a double crate of nails to a shelf three feet over his head, it's only right to do the same thing for the women on the job.

What are you doing under my car, Lady?

If she's wearing greasy cover-alls with her name embroidered over the left pocket, leave her alone. She's just been hired by your dealership or your service station, and you *know* those guys wouldn't have hired her if she weren't damn good.

If she's under your car and she's not wearing cover-alls with her name embroidered over the left pocket, call an ambulance. You probably just ran over her.

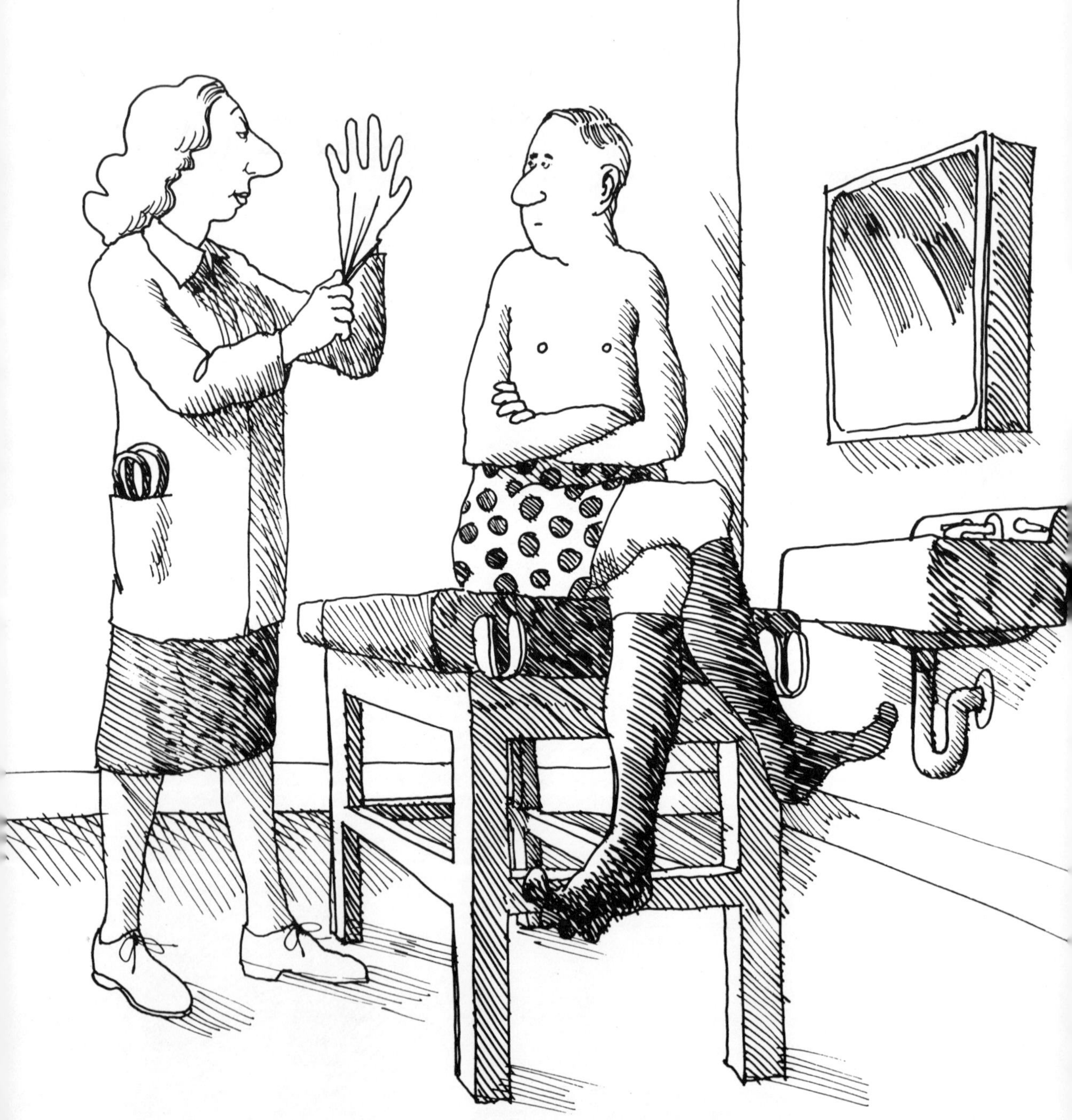

What do you say to a woman doctor?

You say, "Well, Doctor, it hurts me right here whenever I do this."

How do you talk to a woman with an odd job?

Exactly the same way you talk to a man doing something you think is interesting and unusual: you ask her about her work.

Women doing non-traditional jobs really like to talk about some of the interesting experiences they've had. So you don't have to be put off or embarrassed to ask.

If you want to know what it's like for a woman to be a smoke jumper or a chimney sweep, ask. We're pretty sure she'll tell you.

You could also say, "Isn't it nice to see a woman doing this for a change."

She'll think that it's pretty nice hearing a man saying that for a change.

SOMETHING FOR EVERYONE

Give the nice lady your seat.

If the bus is full, and the woman has targeted you to stand in front of, and she continues to glare at you as though she expected to lift you out of your seat by sheer eye contact, it is your decision as to whether her intimidation forces you to your feet. Many women are suffering from the same conditioning you got, and they still expect this of you.

But under most circumstances these days, you can still keep your seat.

Unless. The woman getting on the bus is going to have to stand on her one good leg for the next twelve miles; is awkwardly pregnant, or is carrying home the 1967 through 1971 insurance company files to analyze. You should also offer your seat if she got a senior citizen card punched when she got on, or if she has a lot of children with her.

This works both ways, however. If you're an impaired veteran, carrying the entire after-Christmas inventory from a department store, tugging along a toddler, or just think that you require the seat more than she does, go ahead and ask her for it. All she could say is, "No."

And if she doesn't, you've got yourself a seat on the bus.

My compliments.

Some of the things that used to seem so complimentary aren't any more. Some definite no-no's are:

"You think just like a man."

"You're really smart for a woman."

"Don't you worry your pretty little head about this."

"You're so beautiful when you're angry."

"My, you're so feminine for a career woman."

"She's really got balls!"

And anything that starts out, "This may sound sexist, but..." will.

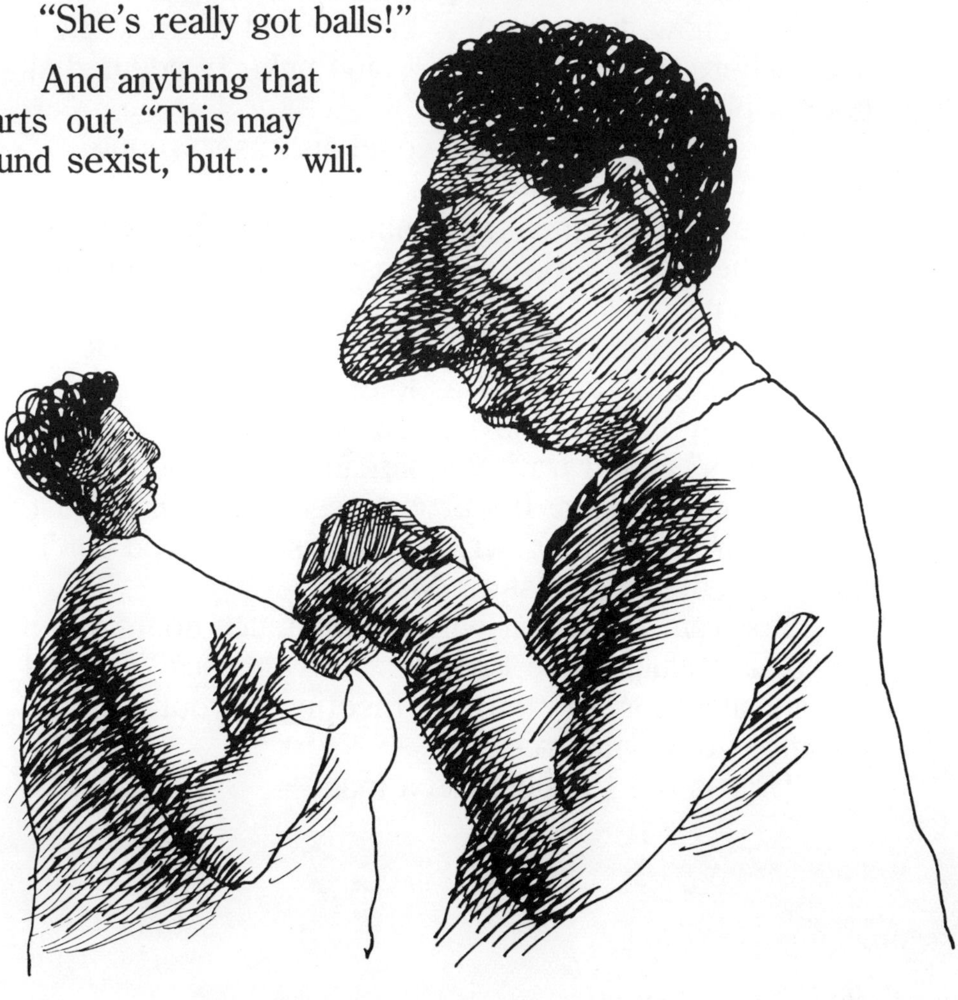

"Now, don't you worry your pretty little head about it."

One giant step for person-kind.

If you're going to use the word "person" as a way to equalize the language, then be sure you use it equally.

Letting him stay a Camera*man,* while she gets herself converted into a Camera*person* sort of defeats the idea that we're all in this together.

Girls or women? Ms.? Mrs.? or Miss?

If she's under fourteen, she's a girl.

If she's over fourteen, she's a woman.

We know it's arbitrary, but we had to draw the line somewhere to make you safe, and puberty seemed as good a place as any.

To be even safer, you could also use "young woman" with the slightly under-fourteens.

The distinction is important because the improper use of the word "girls" could lose you all your enlightenment points.

"Ladies" or "Lady" seems to be coming back into vogue. It's okay to use it as long as there isn't any connotation of white gloves and blue hair.

"Miss" and "Mrs." you already know, but "Ms." may not be so clear. It's pronounced "Miz" and is used most appropriately for writing letters when you don't know whether it's Miss or Mrs.

You can also use it without too much doubt when you're introducing the President of your local National Organization for Women to a meeting of your local Chamber of Commerce.

Unless the President is a man.

13 years, 364 days *14 years, 0 days*

"Boy! This place is crawling with broads!"

"Where'd all the Broads and Chicks go?"

Words like "Broad" and "Chick" have been consigned to the same graveyard where you'll find words like "Nigger," "Spik," "Wop" and "Kike."

For exactly the same reasons.

Authors' note.

There are so many subjects still to be covered. We couldn't conceiveably get to all of them, unfortunately. So if you have a question or a specific situation you'd like some advice on, please write to us in care of Smuggler's Cove Publishing, and we will attempt to answer.

S.R. and F.H.